D0558229

THE SHELL OF WHEN

Also by James Giles

The Way of Awareness: Reflections on Taoist Philosophy (forthcoming)
The Nature of Sexual Desire
No Self to Be Found: the Search for Personal Identity
A Study in Phenomenalism

THE SHELL OF WHEN

James Giles

Windways Press

Lulu.com

Copyright © 2011 by James Giles

Published by Windways Press

Printed by Lulu.com

ISBN 978-1-257-38218-7

All rights reserved. No part of this book may be reproduced
in any form by any means, electronic or mechanical, including
photocopying, recording, or by any information storage and
retrieval system, without permission in writing from the
copyright holder.

This book was printed in the United States of America.

To order additional copies of this book, please visit:

www.lulu.com

CONTENTS

Four

FOREWORD

The very title of *The Shell of When* tells you to expect that the poems collected under it will be singing of corners, crossroads, and quirks. These poems are situated at the unstill point in the whorl of a mollusc where the invisible comes into view, or not quite, where something is dreamed of, or where the sensuous becomes either tangibly sensual or only tangentially sensed like a word about to settle on the tip of the tongue.

The poems of the first group surprise us with snapshots of goings-on: tea-pickers working, rain falling, and scattering spray seen through a lens brightly as though for the first time, sometimes as though from the edge of a cliff, perhaps one of 'the cliffs of time' referred to in a poem of this first group.

Several of the poems of the second group are reminders that the edge of a cliff is a place from which we may fall or leap into an abyss. Here we see through a glass darkly either towards something impending or to something we know not what pursuing us. Here the dreams are 'dreams in hell', nightmares. Here the shell is broken.

The third part of the book treats of what a poem by Paul Valéry calls 'the last gifts and the fingers that defend them'. In the poems by James Giles these gifts are given with a givenness whose temporality, involuted like the spatiality of a shell, obliges him to improvise a new tense in which to say, miraculously, 'I loved her forever in a moment of time'.

The final part brings together haiku-like fragments comparable with shards of a shattered Japanese blue-and-white jug. If night falls in some of the poems of this section, it is a night illumined by the moon or the stars, or a night that falls in the sense of falling away, collapsing, withdrawing into its own deeply secret abyss, eclipsed by the sunrise to which the dreamer awakes.

Predominant in each part are poems of the present participle, poems of the –ing. In them things thing. They are glimpsed in their present or presently happening. Their happening is repeated in the going-on of a traveller. The shell of their when is also the pilgrim's conch of a where that ranges from South Asia and the Far East and the Pacific through the Mediterranean to Scotland and Scandinavia, and from the space of that external geography to the inward space of the journeying poet's caring and caressing imagination.

Acclaimed internationally for his writings in the field of philosophy, no less deserving to be read are the songs of James Giles the poet.

John Llewelyn

ONE

Tracing the Way of the Ancient Heart

If I could trace the ancient ways
and find the moment that thought combines
all in these hands that drift apart
would keep the secret that death unwinds
towards this purpose would creak the door
that opens softly to morning's breath
amid the gardens to stand alone
amid the moment to breathe in death
would withered hands combine the thought
open the secret that keeps apart
morning's purpose that life unwinds
tracing the way of the ancient heart.

SIDEWAYS

Sideways the sun falls
giving way to a blanket
of endless stars
in footsteps at the end of
impressions waiting
to be filled
with sideways glances
briefly cast like echoes
through the mountains
quietly returning.

Starview

Scattered like spray
in a world of caves
winding corridors
racing their way
through endless space
from nowhere to nowhere
through endless time
from ever to ever
spreading through whirlwinds
with no source or no goal
wandering forever
without ever a home.

FIELDS OF GLITTERING SPRAY

There is the sun and there is the grass
a rebound of endless times long past
their prime yet born anew sparkling
mornings laced with dew that was sprinkled
without a plan like scattering days
in opal clouds for the taking as they glide
on their way, parting, dissolving, and melting away
they saunter across their shivering expanse
of myriad fragments suspended in time
over mountains who bathe in their wandering sway
strewn over fields of glittering spray.

THE CLIFFS OF TIME

Over countless years
an instant can take
crossed through the waiting
weaving their way among
the mantle of trees
lifted by the mountains
in the warm summer breeze
whirling before me
there arose in those winds
leaves from the woodlands'
life from the dust
cascading jewels
over the cliffs of time
speckling the journeys
born on life's way
caressing the darkness
in the clear light of day.

CLUSTERS OF LIGHT

Clusters of light falling through the trees
roam across the open sand
announcing their arrival
from distant lands taking back
the ripples the winds had blown
casting them further like chaff in the air
spreading out through the world
each on its own extending their reach
into realms unknown to pierce the shadows
that dissolve in their path and mix and mingle
and move on their way disappearing
in a vapour of sparkling haze.

LEAVING HOME

I left my home
and headed East
but something rose
to stop my feet

I turned to view
the way I came
but every way
was just the same

no way forward
and no way back
while wondrous worlds
called through the cracks.

ALONG THE COAST

Too soon gone
to once miss home
folding hands
I walk alone

along the coast
of silent sky
where clouds drift
and seagulls fly.

SETTING SAIL

A jewelled morn
was mine to hold
I set it on
a tree of gold

and setting sail
within the West
I watched it gleam
and took my rest.

THE SHORES OF CEYLON

Sitting alone
on the shores of Ceylon
I watch the waves lap
from dusk till dawn

and when dawn breaks
with her sapphire light
I watch the waves lap
from morn till night.

EACH WITH HER BASKET

In the tea-fields of Kandy on a wandering slope
they chatted beneath the mid-morning sun
each with her basket and leaves in her hand
they laughed with each other lost in their ways
while wandering clouds waxed and waned
mixing their shadows in the light mountain rain
moving through the bushes they went on their way
picking their tea through the wandering day.

THE PHILOSOPHER'S WALK

In Kyoto I left the Philosopher's Walk
past the time-maker's handles
held by tireless lines
to a clicking from nowhere
tracing out designs in the temple grounds
from wind through their windmills
I took gently to the breeze
and leaned on the window sill and watched
as they eased their way through
the figures in moss-covered stone
standing alone beneath the maples
at Honenin's gate to enter the stream
at the garden's edge letting my feet go
as they went their own way
to a clicking from nowhere
slipping away through warrens
of stillness over carpets of leaves.

THE ROAD TO DATONG

In the village where I had my morning tea
a water buffalo stopped to look my way
before turning to wander off down the road
swinging its tail in its own gentle way
following a trail that left the village behind
the dust from its hooves settling over its tracks
it headed through the rice fields ambling along
making its way to the caves of Datong.

IN THAILAND'S TEMPLE

In Thailand's temple
the wind-chimes sound
amid the branches
nowhere to be found
never mind how hard I try
blue eyes in the guest room
asking me why
I must search for them
'Oh just let them be'
I hear them saying
chiming through the trees
kneeling beside me
her blonde hair reaching down
amid the branches
nowhere to be found.

The morning beach

I watched the monks
on the morning beach
and began to weep
as each by each
passed me by
without a sound
sitting cross-legged
upon the ground.

HAWAIIAN PATHS

Hawaiian paths
through earth-like sun
jettisoned at sea
set their mark on
these ancient shores
amid the swaying trees

I couldn't see
but heard them go
through the taro fields
in searching for
the hula's heart
that swaying hips concealed.

Opunaho Bay

From Opunaho Bay
through the marae heart
I followed the course
of a long lost dart
flung through the jungle
traversing the earth
an island bird watched
while morning clouds burst.

LINDHOLM HIGH

Blazing daybreak
over Lindholm High
sets the stones
in amber frames
lighting the steps
from the fjord below
retracing the journey
from whence they came
on footpaths aglow
with streaming light
wind carrying sand
through the fields.

Swallows over Florence

Swallows over Florence
in the gold of a Tuscany dawn
sunlight shimmering off their wings
as they climb through the echoes
of their pterodactyl calls
whirling through streams in the crystalline air
turning and diving each without care
to skim the tiles of the rooftops below
and once again climb in the beat of a heart
lost in the wingbeats that set them apart
artists of the air whose canvas is the sky
swallows over Florence
painting pictures as they fly.

SOUTH COLLEGE STREET

Walking up
South College Street
quite by chance
I turned my feet
underneath
Port Potter Row's
Bristo Square
where lost winds blow
all was swept
out of my hand
I couldn't say
but only stand
and watch it fade
beyond all hope
slithering up
the Indian rope.

IN MORNINGSIDE

In Morningside
when summer's gone
and morning tea-trays
slide with the eyes
everything writhes
to step anew
to quietly step through
something now that's gone

with the light
of close-lit days
waiting the night
to slide with eyes
that close no more
dripping tea upon the floor
where I in opening try
entering the closing
that softly sighs

among shadow leaves
that cover my walks
through the Meadows
yet leave an infinity
of dying questions
breathed upon the trees.

TWO

Shattered Glass on the Trees

Nothing was left
a trail of blood
shattered glass on the trees
the beating of wings
lifting hard from the marsh
formed reflections in the wind
shuffling the branches, bark, and leaves
rising with the swaying
riding the breeze
loosening at last from the canopy below
hope for a lifetime
waiting for birth
burst by a death knell
returning to earth
loose forever amid the debris.

When morning calls

A hand opened
a nail fell
a heart broken
through dreams in hell
weathered softly
beneath a tree
tarred and feathered
to let it be
a hope to breathe
a hammer falls
breaking the heart
when morning calls.

CHASED AND HUNTED

In the moment of finding
that all will be lost
chased and hunted
through desolate lands
being driven by rains
on a hard winter's night
frozen at the crossroads
of nowhere to go
hounds in the distance
closing in fast.

BROKEN SHELLS

With racing breath
and darting eyes
step by step
the horror swells
looking back
to once held hopes
strewn on the floor
like broken shells
all in the moment
piercing all time
collapsing beneath
the swing of the axe
horror! horror!
rising black sun
hot on the heels
of nowhere to run.

ONE SMALL COIN

Panic on a knife-edge
hacking holes in the door
a fist through the window
an infinity of horror
clawing and choking
in a storm of sand
snatched by the throat
held hard by hands
that spread over ever
palms facing down
dropping one small coin
that never was found.

No signs on the way

Crushed hopes in the mist
clenched hard in a fist
fleeing the fear of
nothing to miss
desperate designs
as trail marks decay
no hope of direction
no signs on the way.

THE SHELL OF WHEN

Blow after blow
a twist of fate
shattered the exit
closing the gate
a gate once open
forever now shut
a shattered bottle
in hands badly cut
from the shell of when
to the core of where
there's room for love
but there's none there
who still could hear
the echo of then
from the core of where
to the shell of when
blow after blow
going down in a spin
falling forever
in a whirl of wind.

THE TWELFTH OF OCTOBER

On the twelfth of October
on a cold autumn day
amid smouldering ruins
of a child's shattered play
I walked down the road
from the hall of dreams
called by the keeper
to paint what I'd seen
when weaving a brush
from the struggle for breath
and dipping it deep
in the darkness of death
I set the stars wide
on a canvas of pain
letting colours run
like blood in the rain
running through ruins
of a life never known
entering the grave
of a child never grown
waiting and watching
each year slip away
on the twelfth of October
on a cold autumn day.

A SUNDIAL OF SHADOWS

In the eve of bereavement when nothing would grow
a sundial waited beneath the snow
where something about her retiring eyes
took me to the precipice
as I watched how the mists
gathered in the antique chasms below
where galloping hooves
resounded through the ravine
trailing life's reins eluding the grasp
in a frenzy of clutching to never hold fast
to a sundial of shadows melting ever below.

A FIRE THAT RAGED

A fire that raged
by the side of the road
like spider's eyes
in the glimmering dawn
who set forth in crawling
through ashes to ashes
in search of prey
that lingered too long
slumped over the wheel
he seemed but asleep
while dripping fingers
giving up the touch
silently hung over
eight legs that creep.

ANIMAL OF LIGHT

The animal of light
rose from the morning streets
like steam off drying clothes.

Where would he find his refuge
in the land soon to be filled with amber knives?

He stopped—the departed years trickled and went
their way never daring to remember
theirs was the lot of love not taken.

Beams of heat shot quickly by
ripping holes in the fleeing night
raising his eyes the veil dissolved.

He was a deadly soul and yet
all about him clung fragments of life
remnants of a journey not taken.

His veins filled with blood
and pushed through the streets
never turning once to see the portals
from a crying sun.

THE MARID MAN

The Marid man
being slow to wake
his hand upon
the world does quake
while all around
the sleeping sphere
in fearful tones
the time draws near
oozing quickens
his elfish eyes
a trembling hand
steadies his rise
straightening fast
he smashes the air
piercing the clouds
his nostrils flare
till taunt and tall
his figure looms
above the earth
his shade consumes
all fowl fall as
his reign begins
fish of the seas
weep in their fins
while all that creeps
upon the earth

returns to dust
the warmth they nursed
and in that flash
of untold fears
the Marid man
then disappears.

THREE

THE KEEPER

I wanted her
and she took my hand
to a harem of dreams
she whispered to the keeper
'I've seen him before'
he nodded and smiled
but still kept the door
I knew that smile
I'd seen it before
reaching out for her
she opened her dress
taking me in her arms
and the warmth of her breasts
sent ripples of waves
on the curtained walls
rousing the keeper
as he whispered to me
'I've seen her before'
I smiled and nodded
and slipped through the door.

Within a Trace

In a far flung corner
of a distant place
her perfume lingered
within a trace
of wondrous longing
as I longed to stay
but in tears moved on
to no other way.

THE RIM OF THE DAWN

I sighed at her smile
and melted away
in swirls of her smell
that dispersed the day
stretching out over
and melting away
on her beautiful hips
that lovingly sway

the embrace of her lips
her bare feet on mine
calmly she's waiting
as forever unwinds
the ways within her
as night streams along
receding in rhythms
on the rim of the dawn.

Away

Away she watches the evening sky
and dawns in the dying light
she yawns with the weight pressed to her heart
to be empty in the hard-pressed night
away she lies in her languid self
a gleam on her slackened lips
yet for all that warmth a shivering tear
creeps from her dream to dampen her hair
so she awakes half missing and rests her hand
on the pillow-side where once would lie
the moonlit eyes midst cloud-like hair
lost in the breath satisfying her ear
once she was here deep in hot arms
white hands holding wet lips to her lap
whispering her love in female gasps
the wayward hair that once swept her cheek
now sways alone. Does she turn in her sleep
or sigh in her dream? Far away she breathes
and the falling breaths like dying leaves
sprinkle over her skin, soft as the breeze
from the closing of a sleepy eye.

OF THE HOLDINGS I MADE

A tremble of winter
through formless days
warm streams of wandering
washing out over the sand
loosening footprints from the paths they betrayed
loosening love like a garment to fade
in the spring of a showing
of the holdings I made
with her I held and her beckoning hair
offered her love as she leaned over me
swept deep through my wonder
and wept in her care her long and lovely and shimmering hair
to my cheek where I held her in the hallway's heart
amid sheets dishevelled where the morning sun shone
sprinkled with petals where we lay on the lawn
and laughed in our love as we whispered away
towards her I watched as she walked my way
pausing before me and adjusting her heels
her nylons whispering between her legs
looking over her shoulder and continuing away
her bra beneath her see-through blouse
magically held in crystal clouds
designing their way over lands unknown
bathing me still in a trickling tear
for her I reached over a table of tea
wrapped in her house-coat

she said I could stay
taking my cup and putting it away
I held her and shivered
each step on the way
and entered her waiting
in a warmth of cares
accepting me softly she
pulled back the sheets
lifting her nightdress
whose lace in the moonlight
forever would fade
in the spring of a showing
of the holdings I made.

WHEN WE WERE ALONE

A mist on the doorstep
crept in as she came
hiding the morning
from minutes that remain
rising from the sofa
I took her porcelain hand
and led her to the dance floor
where our portent began
while everything swung
and moved gently away
encircling our merging
as she moulded to mine
her heart beating firmly
in the depth of my dream
swimming in the glowing
brooks from her eyes
beacons of longing
from her little-girl smile
through the way of her wantings
to the way upstairs
grasping the railing
while clasping my heart
to a realm that leads ever
through uncharted ways
countless and effortless passing away
giving into her softness

in the instant I strained
to find her still there
while her pretty brown hair
swirled through my fingers
like a draught in my hand
streaming ever upwards
to the top of the stairs
in the temple of enchantment
I made with her there
as something within me
took me back to my home
in my moment within her
when we were alone.

An afternoon walk

We walked over the bridge
stopping to gaze at the harbour below
in the afternoon of our longing
for a breeze from the sea
mixing the moment of her and me
clouds shifting from a summer's day
feeling her warmth as she took me away
in the joy of her touch pressed fondly in mine
with the smallness of her hands resting
lightly in line of a movement of nestling
up through her blouse her jumper loosening by itself
as she slid up to recline in the crook of my heart
perfectly fitting her female form
into the furrows of a gathering storm
that carried us through the harbour's channels of time
in the heart of abandoning her heart to mine
pressing upon me with her winsome smile
and her unbearable nakedness
beneath her clothes waiting for the asking
but so gently away asking for nothing
but the asking to stay
in that moment we embraced there
our lives entwined
how I loved her forever
in a moment of time.

We met in the forest

We met in the forest
under a wondering tree
its leaves falling gently
casting wide its dreams
where she turned to enfold me
to collapse in my arms
in the flow of her breathing and the quiet of the day
her perfume played gently wandering away
in the shade of reclining
with the ease of a breath
opening a corner of long-sought together
casting her veil to fall wherever
she took me with the touch of her hand
racing in ways that did not understand
how I held her she smiled with eyes barely closed
how she pressed up against me in the shuffling light
shifting through shadows
that played gently on her thighs
loosening her lips
while releasing her sighs
smothering the tension with the smooth of her tongue
quivered by winds through the dream-spreading trees
taking me gently in the backs of her knees
we floated through rivers of the afternoon sun
swirling through her hair washed in the leaves
entwining my ankles in the currents of breeze

gentle and coursing
through time's hidden ways
gazing through crystal
at the passing of days.

Rain fell on her skin

Undressing in the clearing
rain fell on her skin
naked with calling
each drop within
to murmur with wonder
and course down her arms
diamond-strewn rivers
weaving through forms
out over her tummy
lulled by the wind
pausing a moment
where forever begins
then continuing on
in a blur down her thigh
vanishing forever
in the wink of an eye.

SHE SHOWED ME A STAR

She showed me a star
in the warmth of her lap
and waited to find where
my gaze would be
in the moment she rested
her hand on my knee
whose fingers rose with the rising sun
undoing the buttons
at the back of her dress
she slid her arms through the armholes
while lifting her breasts
and lifted the hair
from the back of her neck
to settle it softly in an instant
to fall out over the ocean
borne by the waves.

WHO KNOWS WHERE

Rustling her fingers
through her long blonde hair
pointing forever
to who knows where
there wailed the wanton
longing the while
watching the whispers
that crept from her smile
carefully coded
so none could know
wondering ever
which way to go
into her eyes
I followed my heart
lost in the softness
that held us apart
shaking with wanting
aching with care
taking her with me
to who knows where.

ON A RIVER OF EVER

On a river of ever
to float on her breath
paddling gently on
the flow of her lips
drifting through backwaters
her dress undone
reflecting the clouds
in the afternoon sun
with the ebb and flow
of the ripples that glide
and fall from her shoulders
in the shade of a tree
leaning out over
our watercourse way
her transforming scent
seeping into the air
to bear me transfigured
to the depths of her being
in the warmth of her womb
while sliding down stream.

WAYS I LOVED YOU

My heartbeat you caressed
my cheek with your breasts
beneath the folds of
your sweet summer dress
your hair in plaits and
your waist next to mine
ways I wanted you
and melted to find
motions your body
was mixing with mine
masking the matrix
we made with our love
fitting together
like hand in a glove
the ways I loved you
I never could say
walking you home at
the end of the day
softly stroking you through
your fluttering dress
while you fondly caressed
my cheek with your breasts.

The Way She Glistened

Rolling in the waves on the island's shore
her uncovered breasts glistened in afternoon's day
streaming with wonder to caress me away
and reaching for my hand with her sky-blue eyes
her bikini shimmered its hues through the spray
clasping her hips with its nylon straps glimmering purple
beneath the fray she laughed and turned and tumbled my way
full and warm in the tropical air her beautiful thighs
lapped by the waves as she crawled up beside me
with her sparkling smile
her white-freckled arms and dripping-wet hair
drenched in the droplets of not knowing where
she placed her face up close against mine
bringing us together from our distant paths
castaways under those East Asian skies
her lovely padded thighs pressing lightly on mine
to a fresh and open world where things shimmered anew
through diaphanous layers of life's chosen ways
travelling in rainbows where I sighed to say
the way she glistened in afternoon's day.

FOUR

Breaking waves

Her gaze flowing on
wanders out over the sea
waves break on the shore.

Meeting

Sweeping through the room
eyes that meet briefly
flame in the nightfall.

Her gaze

The flaming stars climb
as she lowers her gaze
igniting the mist.

Fullness

Parting crescent lips
the moon shimmers in fullness
calling me to her.

Brushing her hair

Slipping off her bra
she turns towards the mirror
while brushing her hair.

Afterglow

Warm hands caressing
in the unspoken afterglow
shimmer sheets of night.

First touch

Swirled her curving neck
she settles her cheek on mine
ancient lands appear.

First steps

Taking the first steps
footpath fading in the rain
her gaze glitters still.

On a mountain path

On a mountain path
I gaze back from where I came
blossoms sprinkle down.

Evening Comes

Dripping fell
lost in the sun
a thousand steps
evening comes.

Koi

A koi in the daybreak
winds through its pond
calmly gliding
on its ancient fins
turning to ask me
where life begins.

Praying Mantis

A praying mantis
on an old stone wall
watches as I pass
from birth to death.

Dragonfly

The dragonfly
of my tears
hovered over
a hatching swan
with shimmering eyes
and then was gone.

SWAN

A swan that lands
in the palm of my hand.

FROM THE SAND

Silently a lizard
creeps from the sand
curling to sleep
in the palm of my hand.

DRIFTING

The dragonfly drifts
in the warm summer eve
watching winter come.

WINDING SWALLOWS

Winding swallows spin
leaving traces on my eyes
swallowing the dusk.

LEAPING

Leaping but slowly
a heron leaves for the sky
wings fanning my heart.

Autumn

In autumn leaves fall
calmly to the forest floor
steam climbs from my breath.

Stillness

In the breathing trees
stillness of a drifting leaf
taking me away.

Whispers

Wind through the branches
passing the forgotten leaves
whispers on its way.

SPECKLED SHADOWS

Speckled on the moss
patterned beams trace their shadows
leaving me behind.

GUAVA FORESTS

In guava forests
water falls to mist and spreads
its veiled rainbows.

TUMBLING FREE

Wandering pebbles
tumbling free in the stream
mingle and move on.

HUSHED

Hushed in emerald morn
steam weaves paths through the jungle
turtle dives below.

MOUNTAIN STREAM

Lotus of my heart
spreading on the mountain stream
droplets from the moon.

NIGHT WIND

Wind with faces sweep
slithering in vacant night
collar loosely blows.

STARS SHINE

Stars shine in my midst
calmly calling eyes of night
whisper up my sleeve.

NIGHT GREETING

A cold door handle
greets me in the empty night
silent stars look on.

WAKING

Waking from a dream
moonlight sprinkles on the floor
welcoming me home.

* 607331-821971 *   4